A Christmas Collection

BOOK 2

Kenon D. Renfrow

The Christmas season is filled with traditions as family and friends gather together to celebrate this favorite time of year. Sharing this wonderful season through music is a tradition that lives on today.

A Christmas Collection contains both sacred and secular holiday favorites. The arrangements include a variety of styles ranging from lush to lively. These beautiful new renditions of well-known Christmas songs are sure to become a tradition with both students and teachers alike.

Contents

Angels We Have Heard on High	19
As Lately We Watched	12
First Noel, The	22
Here We Come a-Wassailing	4
Holly and the Ivy, The	2
Patapan	10
Toyland	14
We Wish You a Merry Christmas	6
What Child Is This?	16

Copyright © MCMXCII by Alfred Publishing Co., Inc.

Cover art: Carol Hamilton
Cover design: Martin Ledyard
Art direction: Ted Engelbart
All rights reserved.   Printed in USA.

The Holly and the Ivy

Traditional
Arr. by Kenon D. Renfrow

Here We Come a-Wassailing

Old English
Arr. by Kenon D. Renfrow

We Wish You a Merry Christmas
Theme and Variations

Traditional
Arr. by Kenon D. Renfrow

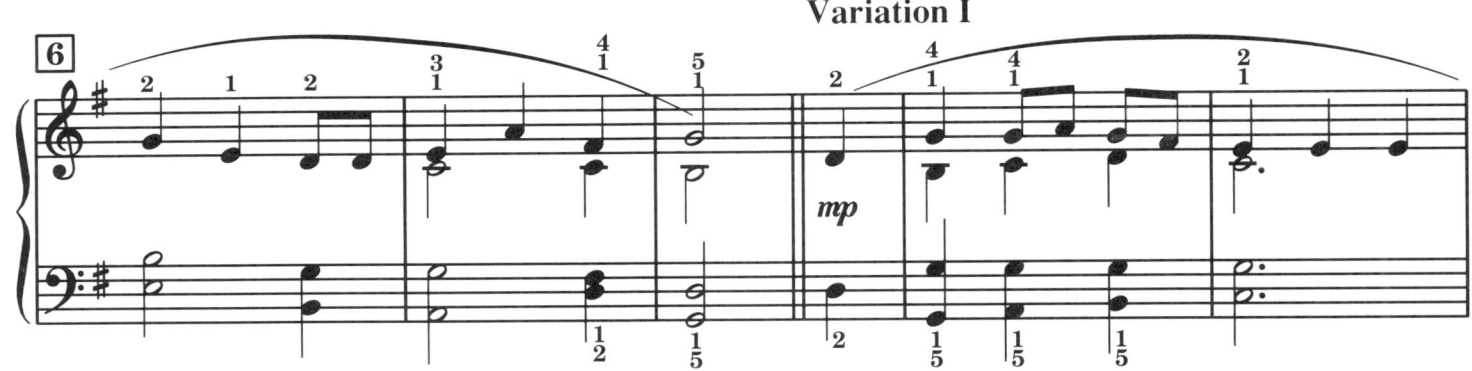

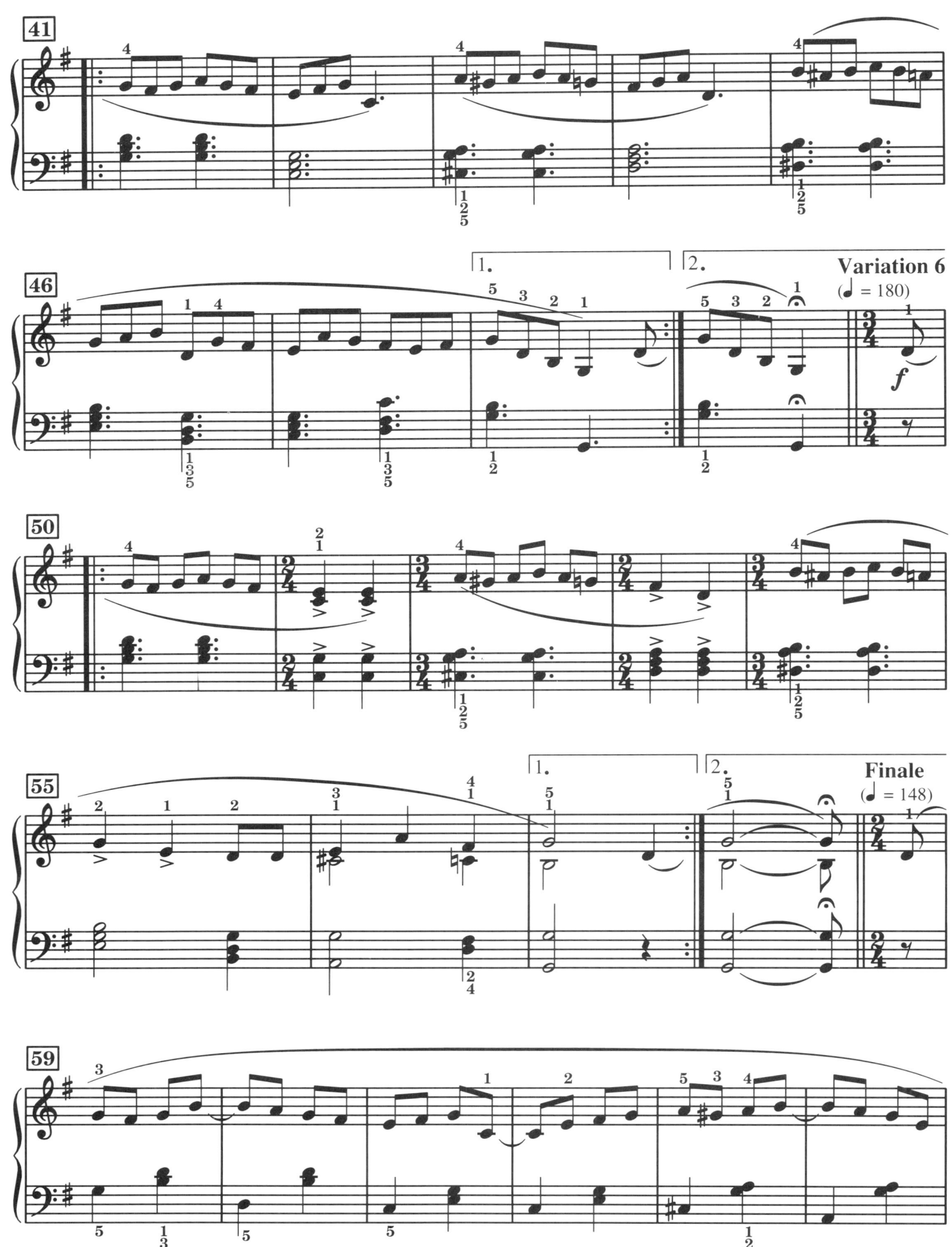

Patapan

Burgundian Carol
Arr. by Kenon D. Renfrow

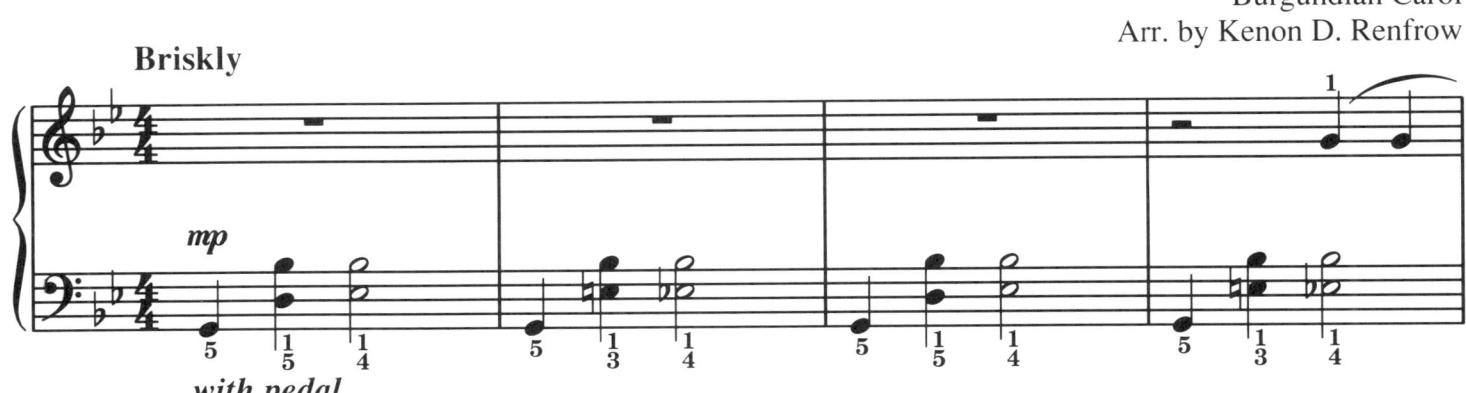

As Lately We Watched

Austrian Folk Song
Arr. by Kenon D. Renfrow

Toyland

Victor Herbert
Arr. by Kenon D. Renfrow

What Child Is This?

English
Arr. by Kenon D. Renfrow

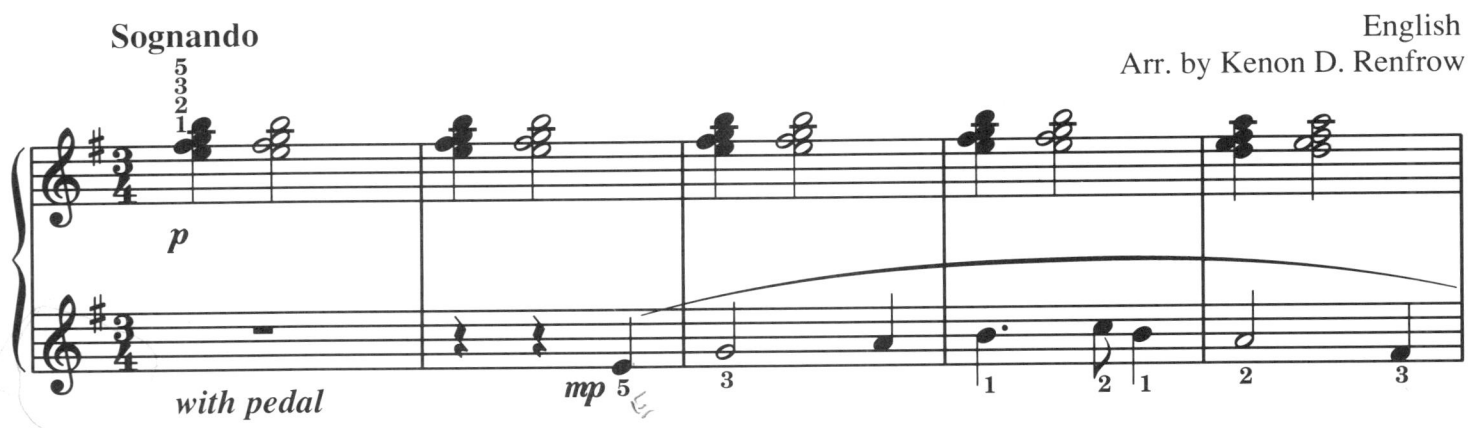
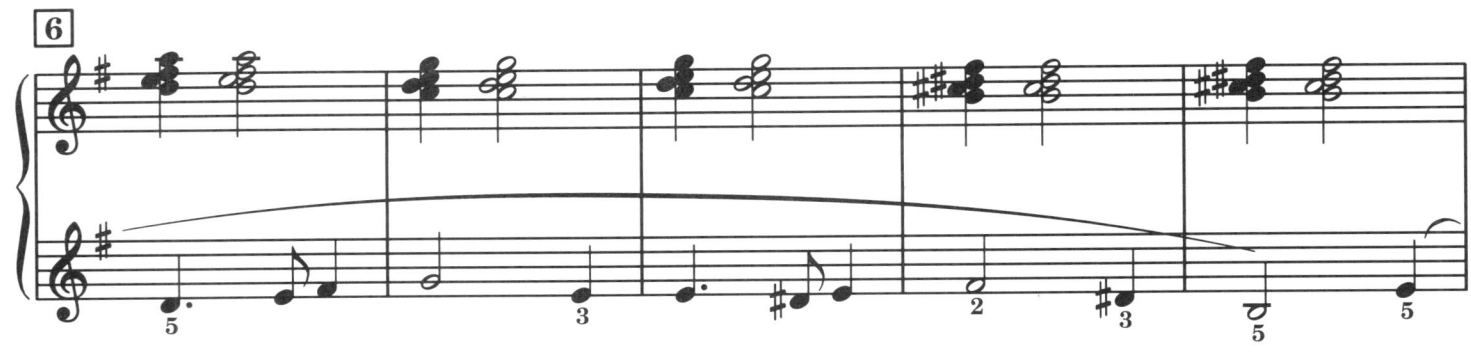

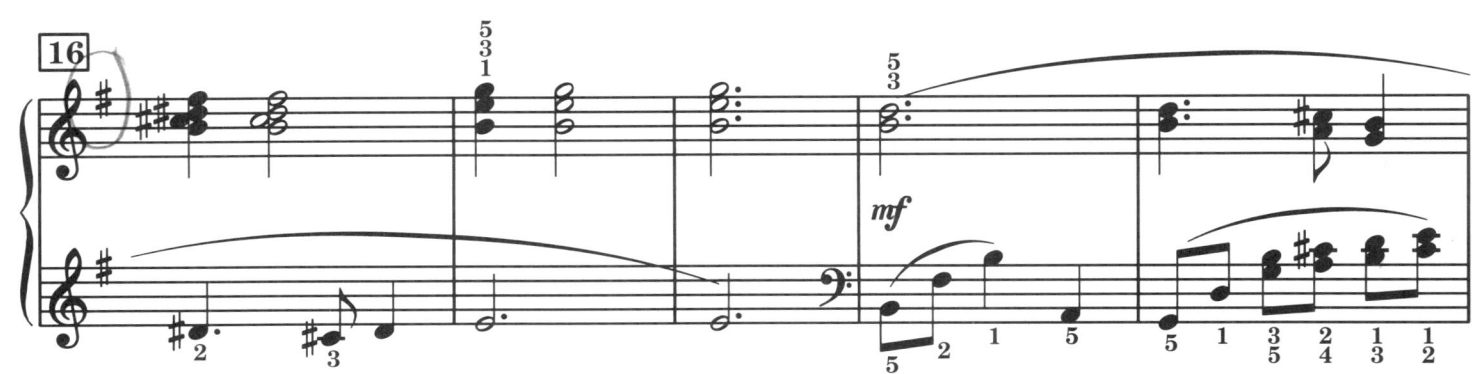

Angels We Have Heard on High

French Carol
Arr. by Kenon D. Renfrow

The First Noel

English Carol
Arr. by Kenon D. Renfrow